Continuity Girl

By the Same Author

Secrets of Elegance, Detroit River Press, 1981
Pornē, In Camera, 1984
Coat of Arms, Station Hill Press, 1992
In the Name, Past Tents Press, 1994

Translation (with George Tysh)
Julie or the Rose by Guillaume Apollinaire, Transgravity Press, 1978

CONTINUITY GIRL

Chris Tysh

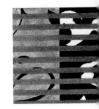

United Artists Books

Grateful acknowledgement is made to the editors of the magazines in which some of these works first appeared: *Chain, Dispatch, Fifth Estate, Hambone, Lipstick 11, Long News: In the Short Century, LVNG, Melancholy Breakfast, Michigan Photography Journal, Poetics Journal, The World*.

The author wishes to thank Wayne State University for a Summer Research Grant which provided precious time during which a portion of this book was completed.

Design by Brian Schorn

Cover painting by Janet Hamrick
Photography by R. H. Hensleigh
Collection of R. H. Hensleigh and Chris Aquaila

Author photo by George Tysh

ISBN 0-935992-10-3
LIBRARY OF CONGRESS CATALOG CARD NUMBER 99-076539

This book was made possible by a grant from The Mushka Kochan Fund.

Contents

for the diasporic
for the exilic
for the displaced
for the ones who cross borders
for G. who moves with me

›Disappearing Series‹

In this glum desert, suddenly a specific photograph reaches me.
—Roland Barthes

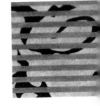

Photo Opportunity

Not exactly burning, the room she slept in
suggested tears as if only a few seconds ago
there had been someone, stepping in from the street
about to extinguish his cigarette, maybe reach
down into her old wicker trunk of opulent phantasies,
a red light impossible to photograph. Look this way,
please. Better move the cat and drop the pretense.
Coffee stains color a silverprint commissioned by absence.
You know the unsorted bric à brac of pet owners,
early school morning light in mesh with same. She reshoots it,
down to the last space between chair and table. Pale enough
to summon a taxi, then slip the telling. It would always
derange, a narrow angle of blame.

Part-Object

He saw it happen before she had looked
into the camera. A whole parade of it, lined
with pedestrian thanks not to be her. Hand-to-mouth,
there are words for this tournament. To bandy about
the frenzy of the visible is simply redundant.
Her eyes, incomparable brakes on the avowed watching.
Summer or winter, she'd stand long enough to be caught
in the frame. It is taken for granted something
will escape him, undecipherable and punishing,
to the end. Sharp block letters returned
to their whiteness. The viewer's privilege obscures
a given field. A brief war of position ensues.
He scarcely dares to arm, awed by the sudden lack of distance
that comes with the terrain, her involuntary smile, mannish coat.
When the flash explodes, the gaze drops,
the staring spent, overexposed.

In One Hour

It will be settled. I could agree
you have lost all sense of proportion.
Such a blur that even told you remain
in the dark. They say application of speed
hardens muscle, white froth recognition
that objects appear more desirable
in the distance. And vice versa. Such fellow-
travelers. Keeping close to phantom mountains
you walk as if in a dream, recognizing in a flash
that sudden arc of light. Did you know we screamed
just before passing go? All sorts of bends grace
the tunnel like a motor gunned to death.
His chances ruined in advance, a man
calls for light to come around and climb the set,
the one with heart-shaped peaks. I'll say nothing
about the way you look into the night.

Brain Noise

Maybe I should mention it wasn't an actual
photograph at all. When the yellow let loose,
the audience pulled its fear like a summer net.
After reciprocal beamings I was left holding
the bag of reddish plumes. At the hippocampus gate
noise subsided, admitting an intermittent sob piano,
electric and formal. Something refused to be
throttled in found objects, derelict beauty held
upside down, the better to batter. Later, felt strips
of symmetry will have dragged on concrete floor,
where blue established residence. Montage glistens
on everyone's lips. I allow the sentence its modicum
of docility, teasing out spider webs, now thick with
struggle. Chalk markings correct our stance.
The thing hangs naked. You tell us.

Double Take

You tip the question back to a period
of anesthesia when the emblematic horn
returns overflowing with numerals.
Bundled up into the fictitiousness of point of view,
a camera shoots at a room. It could hurt
the facts, more painful than stated in the familiar
lecture on composition. A simplest sheet of blue
rain whose nature consists in blocking other referents
will spread and enter into production of meaning:
a solitary dark figure at work on his desire
to see. To tumble, these polygons, defer
closure, beneath them, a smooth multiplication
table extends into floor and scrambles
this particular narrative we hastily assemble
to be done with watching, eyes closed
to the slow mechanisms that fool us into pressing together
the nervous slant of packaged goods, xeroxed weather.

for Carl Toth

⟩Blue Archive⟨

The frame fits badly.

—Jacques Derrida

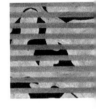

Tankard

same darn light
that swivel,
hooked arm in front of coach a bandaged
head maintains ground, scraping glass
the desire to break from feminine impediment
the one with yellow-green pieces: jars,
flasks, inkwells, two white tankards
who knows what's in the bucket. To the left a rag
bone man enroute mourning suit, the woman
in white, threading and lily-pad. Too pale
at that, blown in obedience with her background
status. Chair or bust, it invites difference.

gaslit street posts odds
rag & bone man drives panel
marked the good shepherd.
"My bucket," she says of the picture.

Columbine

petty pettish fetish unvest
saucy sweetheart to the rescue
almost has eyes pewter made
to gutter tears, the largeness of her pores
usurps my position as either outside,
tantara! travelling hands shore up

the decorative past or present connivance
with moribund standard for measuring
the margin, borderline X of Y, the labile
nightmare that accompanies every painting.

small troops translate
rope off any intervention
into the sequence of events,
diese Kinder, this little girl

Coach

not the nightmare that accompanies every painting
but talismanic endurance, an artist to herself
I would say has eyes hair black quail,
a sense of being prey. Not the chubby shoes
nor the morning light, the way the vest flops
to make provision for the crypt where lies the dead
object on the canvas: white coat real heavy shoes
like a system of disturbances credits the bottom
band, must be repeated against the ear of the other.
To consort with the world of pure exchange, nine
squares detail punctuation marks, the more residual
contents frame shirt lift dress, always a disfiguring
moment: the little pair with eyes of early ruin.

she's standing on a pedestal or part of it.
Red bucket black wheel no longer moving
on coals, gutted undone dismembered
in the Western stance

Bandbox

like wallpaper I had the impression
what counts as history & its humiliation
skip a phase I won't say stick
their butts out or throw in the towel
walking away, the well is there, she
already knows it is a question of resemblance
not the same bloody chamber or fifth child
delivered from maternal tongue, a section
of ruby coach painted at top speed
fills in the future shrinking rose trellis

the place from which they're facing us
preempts narcissistic version, *der Nabel-*
schnur looms large in the mirror
he would mug for. Catwalk exit.

Charger

all the same the banality of arguing retains.
Sink sieve defer fund or who knows what
schizophrenia descends from her. Cropped frame
will trigger that exaggeratedly thin waist, that is
a length of hair caught in the wheel we've drawn
there. In that sense a spit of land fears copper,
bête grise or lack of surface pinions its holder
to the country of last things. At first stab
a missed beachhead later pop anatomy black
sheen scramble to press the painting we saw
in reverse: wanted erased after the fashion of X

if you were to lack & then
return verging on a tall tale
sienna charger in the title
shaky yellow of a barricade

⟩Acoustic Room⟨

The sound of the words is sometimes
95% of poetic presentation.

—Louis Zukofsky

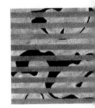

Green Eyes

Have him voyeur, main tenant, common paver. Yes-Verse is completely
redesigned. A plate. Jules, toupee varsity sat on depressing tomb hour,
dim tile. Too few touch her. Main floozy fiesta, I'll knee
federate Peter Passgrand, choose pork quiche, rebound issue, heavy acraze!
Restitute domain service guards. Was Vinny's sister, Amy,
veritably discovered? May's mafia was, gee risk Danny Pavoul pardoned.
Was a vesuvian courage dismounted? Many cry pancake rest here in moreso.
Yes-Verse vase remit. Yes-Verse had ditched a train, desiring ain't easy.
Jimmy reconstrue. Jimmy reefer anew. I, divine pilferer, cane chatterbox.
Pilferer, kale fortress. Was man tender? Jesus, the fortress! Dance,
my cells, jeopardy cuss toads, vowels, sold it, billiards. Mafia was!
Ginseng pass, sure key, my guardians and my chains purr less, continue
seize latch cunt revue! Iliad's sentinels surmise shamans drained.
Iliad's spying on the party. Jesus, the fortress and Jesus, solo mondo.

Beware! I'm not sure that my guards and my dogs can contain them if I let
them loose on you! I've got ropes, knives, ladders! Beware! There are watchdogs
on my rounds. There are spies everywhere. I am the fortress and I am alone in
the world.

after the French of Jean Genet, *Haute Surveillance*. Paris: Gallimard, 1949, pp. 71-72

Second Chant

All on, Sultan, evoke two languages, debar us, my dizzy song key, sail
it o'er the parquet. The bandage is fine: man, front attention, hate
to lovey away; deal o Sally, edgy crossy, this bandolier, a travesty
of my visage. The result at nest pass infinite. Quart shimmies, places
of sand and dixie moochers. Any quarrel passes, a première aboard,
K Maldoror contains a tent design with dense arteries; car chassis figure,
numbril Kelly's reflexes due cadaver. Mess infant, set Tecumseh.
Pewter quay set up pray tool and song, kaput, continue sans corpse and
illest, probably kill neon rest passbook. Assay, assay, Cheyenne avid;
lest the parquet tell kill it; to us Levant ramp lit. Any faux pas
contains deboarding; cartoon tar dress pays off me. To us convent meant
refuge, vatic cushy, dance in a channel; esteemed nature, densely boner;
car tune pants wrap us, alley fame, pending trust jury's immense
grace aglow, bulky t'is, send dues, dent on, sir, a vicuña
satisfaction sullen meant visible. Toy Leman, prance ballet; I would
ray ocean prin her on; may Johnny pass the force.

Come on, Sultan, with your tongue, get rid of this blood that stains the floor.
The dressing is done: my forehead dried and washed with saltwater, and I have
crossed my face with bandages. The result is not infinite: four shirts full of blood
and two handkerchiefs.

after the French of Isidore Ducasse, Comte de Lautréamont, *Les Chants de Maldoror*. Paris: Garnier-
Flammarion, 1969, p.84

Eden Eden Eden

/Less sordid, caskets' jambs over foul muscles retain us;
nouveautés in maillots; dance, shall we? Carla T, Violet: lest babies
rule hordes, brassy femmes & acre of pies, sorely tall maître d' of the
GMCs; the chauffeur reposes away, something libertine, shafted project,
dense cabin; école Ferkouss, a section of RIMA traverses the pistol;
the soldiers sought or decamp; two of RIMA seek couch on the cairn, the test
approved contrary to cribbled silex, daypin denudes the host, delirious
corpse, umbrage in the guardroom; fame's berth: less babies, country
lessons; the movement dispersed, removes rain forces; parlor sewer
incident; perfumes don't lure high on, lure pulls, lure chairs scent,
impregnate: we'll jeer off any boor indigo, suffer dainty main—at the base
of Ferkous, soul apron charged with cedar's calcined orgy, bless rushers,
tombs, buffet echo get us, figures meshed to merits, too pissed, flowers,
pollen, abyss, brine papers and tough macule delay, demur, D sang,
E course, plumes,

/The soldiers, helmeted, legs apart, with flexed muscles, trample
the newborns swaddled in scarlet shawls, violet: squatting on corrugated
iron, machine-gunned by the GMCs, the women let the babies roll out
of their arms;

after the French of Pierre Guyotat, *Eden, Eden, Eden*. Paris: Gallimard, 1970, p.15.

Country of My Dreams

The reply dangles, dissipates, dunked scissors of decision in balance.
Gem trove, I sir, entire labor, a weekly solely at my dread, and am a gaucho,
ladies, somber vale of vultures, key fillet parallel to silos, back riven
at the direct index, crave ass, partly magnetic thistle.
This atoll reveals it, din shack, cellular atmosphere. Lesser desert,
coping lair, common vitriol essay; darling ales of silage incandescent.
Mess palms, definite dealers' perch, part silence diffused and perfect
lune of vultures glistened along dune, ray on; looming serrate enters
his griffes. Saddest scent, rectilinear conduct amain, dread-killed
charade; back event to remount rejoinder. The troupe kiss, approach
it, vertiginous men on the horizon.
The map pursues B & T, caged, immobile, tired, turning south, mass
pied and the others' dawn; grand Capella's fiendish mane, tenor man,
haughty. Gin fences the horizon, commie mirrors in succession; chuck
one of my pies postdance, a silo commissar wets the rail and the guard
fixed in the cilia of vultures.

I'd break through horizons like successive mirrors, each of my feet
down in a furrow which served me as a rail and my eyes fixed on the trail
of vultures.

after the French of Michel Leiris, *Haut Mal.* Paris: Gallimard, 1943, pp. 22-23.

Love of a Mortal

An ego said sovereign, come here, nounou, anchor us, commoner sufferer.
Satinette chair, lacrosse insignia said to lower trash, human daily amour
and daily sufferance. Kitty de Chirico meant this genus, the mystique's
pretty handy in the temples, hold the fire. A leisured ally, plus lane.
Carry a savant lip over, defer the grand fitting like a plain response;
is it set and due, kin apply, nil form, nil mode. Menace nail us, play loin.
K convenes, parity debut. Jam is noon deviance, oblique effusion, divinest
approach of the human, kill all proceeds. Selene's dominion, dock in fashion.
Said Pluto the contrary case's free. Carjack race, could you dance, *this instant*,
the effusion quasi humble in spirit, too sultry, ditch'er, remains profound kitsch
calvary, the final adieu: epithet, the sense deals a mere divine idyll,
dine us, don her; the press' sentiment, daily men city continued
paramour, damn it, mortal. Lame or human, amen, please grant, silliest
only, deny us, deign assurance, alien purloin, kill, instant maim,
and din us an appeal to cheers, the irrepparable desire meant.

It is a being of flesh, bleeding upon the cross, it is the very human
horror of death and suffering which the mystic perceives through
the rending of his knees at the moment he collapses. He may go further.

after the French of Georges Bataille, *L'Amour d'Un Etre Mortel*. Paris: Ludd, 1990, p. 26.

⟩Continuity Girl⟨

There is a cost in every identification.

—Judith Butler

adam's apple

why she ain't had meat yet when some had
gravy as well
he asked in the visiting hours' inquisitive

whine. Suck job & sandwiches later she turns
a corner wraps one
demures. Her sense of debt to larger doubts

carries speed pocket knife to shadow in the blue
archive between shifts
no tatter tale to read on the arm so tipped it sinks

in the lay of summer this open house of stress syllables
about to slap
a square canvas she'd take to trick the eye

eclipse

that the doctor nodded and a bed
went down so far north past the last

reason of madness like the rash period
when he took her dozing under the derelict

netting. The slide to pair fraud with black
pumps, body of another woman in the installation

night hammers at the chassis, jumps
history strutting between parts. What will happen now

in this flip reading you go smash against the glass
license, begin walking into her bedroom like a man

qui dort debout dans la nuit du chasseur, wouldn't
support the possessed laughter of those who lost, much less

sink down over and against a buttered surface. The surrender
of sleep requires watching the unendurable demolitions

la guerre des pronoms

which recalls the conspicuous absence of men

which brings out the warrior in them, volcanic
column up to their hair

which they say, a hundred of them in a certain state
of mind will summon from the old sentence

crowded in the gutter, they lash out tongues
and shrieks to take him at his word, tail in a trap,
it goes like that

halte-là! who wrote the slogans, advance publicity
inserts young women, some wounded with instructions
to jump X, crown O, the rest written sideways
needs less distance, their eyes tear
with laughter

whose license was lost later in the day, Perdita

would bolster pedestrian access, nodding
acquaintance with nightwood bodies
if you know that pell-mell oblivion
that consensual congress to slot
out of cramped space, irritating meaning

in massacre

table ladies who cut the kind of yawning
mouth, moire silk matins off the block

December never could understand whence came
the ineluctable panic of novices, House of Pain

words are extracted in procession, black habit
and scarf, Mariette practices distress, wide

stitches angle down inside her, the better to skein
three sisters in a pew given the crown or lashes

any morbid condition arising from veiling the question
of corporality, surfeit hand towel reddens in chapter

room, our prioress calls mud-colored, you'd have to
whisper. Psalms. Speech. Wild grass, beds

of cherry wood. Postulant vamps, handsigning in half-
mittens. Do you suppose you could, one by one

in your own words tell us about the roses on her palms

matrix

it did not help to know that
in the history of shame there could
never be a precise referent one rallied to

like ground troops erasing the distance between discourse
and thing. The description of Rani's shawls
embroidered more precisely than newsreels denounces

the fiction of a benevolent father
neither soldier nor sage when it comes to bomb
motherland. With idle vouloir-dire advanced

as cleavage, three mothers impossibly tall collapse
all difference. Am I right in saying, pushed up
like a demi-bra? to bind together this capricious

clinamen toward decamping in the narrow sense.
Rather than table the matter, they inaugurate the body's
abeyance, an elusive practice of barter with the hangman.

Held in reserve, large black cloth descends
via rickety dumbwaiter, untouched remnants really,
that signal the dubbed dialogue of death

for Salman Rushdie

period

apart from numb you will have siphoned off
                              "Miss must not get upset"
years behind pinafored ellisions, crabbed
                              "Yes, daddy"
phantom roaming across the flat veld
sooner or later the plaster will dry
                              "Stop it, I scream"
while the one who lies hears a shuffle step
lame tread of the would-be kin

That must be how the ruinous snatch
                              "Take off those clothes at once"
lends credit to free indirect speech
                              "the fishy smell of her"
bottoms up. That too she squanders, lacking
common ground with the mob
                              "more, he whispers"
like dregs, I, the corrupt matter
remain   "please, don't be cross"
untranslated

impossible

lassitude, neither of us
not reprimanded, not dead yet
conveys the scene to be filmed tomorrow.
Music at the cut and in the upheaval
bound to follow, consoles
for the loss of ego one could never show
without destroying that mouth, flush
joint with duplicate pieces on display.

We are weeping.

Whole days pass in slumber. Were the exchange
to take place, we would begin at the boundary
of a complete sentence. This is unavowable desire.
A woman puts me to bed. Useless to describe her.
In the counterfeit pose she assumes, none
of the words can be traced and yet,
what uproar charivari alarum we make at night
to divide the dead from the living, head first
into noon-blue gutter, unscripted fall.

shanghai

        broadened to include funereal piers
which is to say not the slit already suspect
that opens up in the paddy fields but the camp

itself, unrelated to forgetting from soldier
to prisoner passing his hands from truckfloor
to water without even a hint of what must be

told one day: the body that burns in advance
jams, at the skin, the shortwave crackle of these events

        that it seek place on rolled up scroll
as marker or history depends on the economy
of knowing. Slack motor across the compound.

Gangs, sentries and flies like a camouflage
matinée cut up before the squatting crowd
framed and separate from the letters of war

by a running fence, its barbed meaning
not yet trenchant nor plain

124 (Bluestone Road)

an intuition backs away, undressed
outside this subject; abject, gestural.

Soda crackers and slop jars in the heap.
"Make her remember!" Fugitive be a way

to get close to it when her water breaks
loose. Still doubtful that ain't her story

firetree or no firetree scorched into back.
Shed something by river's edge, to name

into being a body disallowed by all. "What
she do that for?" Reverse that sentence,

lest baby ghost start a storm, fix
meaning after the handsaw. "Soleil cou coupé."

bottom

Turned on itself the body politic gives way to symptoms.

Sumptuary laws hang on a single shred of evidence.

Found frigid in his dream about dissection.

I knew it once from the awry prelude.

Each novel savages its audience in advance.

Like a tonal syncope or tomb we walk over

citing the convention of denial. An imbecile in moonlight.

You recoup the circuit in mock concession to desiring machines.

Get up and go as if force relations equal red carnation.

Pink façade or whores older than it makes out under the boardwalk.

cimarrón

measured in rum
                        the coded romance
of belonging nowhere
                        rattles lurching inside
its moving frame
                        at once the presumed ramp
threatens heat returns
                        to faster rhythms. She is tired
of explaining the etymology
                        I hear it now: ska yellow fufu
sucking teeth in
                        between bites

To screen events out of order
                        like reaching the sea before lightning flash
conjures a spectral body
                        against scummy water
"castration ain't de main t'ing"
                        something further inland
not so much usury
                        as imperial portion gone to bush
deep in high ruinate
                        blends a case of dynamite

I shot the sheriff
                        that hollow sound when falling
shrapnel in place of tarpaulin
                        Come to Jah bredda
blackened dream island
                        colors the margin
dub for the rest of us

passing

though collapsed, bundle
in hand: I repeat

our names by the window
assembled like bedbunks

neighbor to neighbor
informed on, a crowd

of girls in rags be waiting
for us. Don't write

barracks lit with omens
such a beautiful hat

as if there was nothing to it
neither border nor river

to cross, hail Mary full of grace
empty platform in the morning

the world of appearance

were he to wear a wire
pitch a tent toward love

then hangdog itch for months
or die in agony, the balance

stopped as if with cork
he will be saved from the water

farewell sentence in his mouth

for Robert Glück

absolute

devotional tinderbox laid out sweetly
on private grounds: a well of tears
adorns her form, meal ticket, an afterthought

this alone tames the mass trapped in its own
ham lechery and wig story, stirs the pot
place like gender, mattress to their tongue

veiled and grinning he rims from memory
to second the motion of her saintlihood

descente de lit

nostalgia's detachable value pops open
where I hang far from home
finger on the buzzer

slow to rise a half-baked heroine
jots her dream on a mystic pad

anonymous as a row of cans, his shtick
goes nowhere: CLOSED FOR REWRITING

window question modeled after
blue collar primer for that phrase
with dangling modifier

masturbating the burglar broke
into her bedroom

for Gail Scott

if you were a girl, he said

hot to trot in a tux of possibilities
one's rice dream raises a sweat

papersack she clasps on the empty stairs
taken by a hunger around his eyes

no blood oranges no hunter sausage
will assuage the terrible carnal fan

fair trading or obsolete murder in a spin
cycle where the surgeon's hand fades to white

stalls reflected in the butcher knife this dumb reversal
wipes the floor uneven to begin with, wrings out the whole

from male to female, limp from ether
a pure rag in the gutter of want

(banality of) heaven

to raise the bar on obsession deposit more
than you'll need—spare tire caution
won't ferry you across if it should come
to pass in a fiery gondola, a peony for every thought

in the interest of satori she had herself pierced

having no choice but to wake up in the men's section
fluff roll stuck on the cut & gauzy conviction pinned
to the chart that dry throat & illegal (meat) traffic
go hand in hand

like scratch artists, you sample each (box) sex—
kismet—before the law delivers—return to sender—
its adjucating address: grapevine double hustle step touch
impassive, fate's fat cocotte calls out the shots

catherinewheel

and
in
one
orgasm
they
came
undone

below
the elastic
lexicon
of
baby
and
bath

for Aaron Shurin

accost

provocation forms a queue, eyes wise with grift
      at the beach casino white and ribbed the little shits
            in wifebeaters enter frame that a language be found

later that day a tangle of handcuffs deforms the shot
      down to her petticoat studded tongue she worries
            like a charm bracelet

off camera scan balcony for spittle yank chain
      pressed to desire's penury wretched facts
            lost and found thumping around her wrists

sleaze winches hoist fantasy up in the air for all to see
      where a chorus of maybes has it out
            hand to mouth in a flash

let's pretend the forbidden object can be had
      under the sidewalk the seashore hails us syntax intact
            light meter still working

showgirls doublepark on bottom screen poofy hairdos
      like clouds in a pasture wrap cheesecake to go
            thin film of habit secure in place with poverty's barrette

peau douce

in punishment for having cast her lot
festooned with headlines leaders and weather
of strain there & then had she been able to
take a hint insinuate herself into a pair
of spike heels on the next train straighten that
black seam as if she'd done little else all lifelong

under the circumstances a shakedown buys alibi
pack of camels after tunnel's hairpin curves
wreck her claim to calm a taste of ashes above the rack

inveterate optimist night scabs over while we die
a little each time we cross the border into blue skin red eyes

⟩Dead Letters⟨

We are quite simply dealing with a letter
which has been diverted from its path; one whose
course has been prolonged, or, to revert to the
language of the post office, a dead letter.

—Jacques Lacan

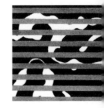

Dear X

The faux intimacy of the you. Insistent, that thin line of saliva
during sleep. As if you were a doctor, blotting this descent
with writing paper or sand.

Arcade or slaughterhouse dream?

The alms of the night dole out a riddle. Sadistic in origin,
the word passes sentence, up and over, swallows chronology.
Rising from sandbox, the dreamer takes account of the middle
window, pulls at the handle, three in the back two in the head.

Dear X

You must have known she'd miss the train, forget
to look at lit up signal. Hair slicked back, narrow
pied-de-poule skirt, not yet the noir cliché of punk.

I suspect lapping hierarchy, a long take subject to proxies.

On the prowl underground ripped out of my mind:
you hold the plain cup of denunciation like a glossy
proof or blowup. In truth you've scanned the wrong text again.

Les colmateuses du système (ideological sealers).
Sewer rats and talking heads, the revenge fantasy that slam
dancing grants us, pinning those bitches against the frame.

Dear X

So what if Jacques said a letter always arrives, etc.?
Two dykes in a dinghy or the post crunch of hidden vantage
point? Let us assume yours is bigger than mine, as if container
for thing contained could mute this line of escape.

In the last instance, a man jumps ship. He will learn
to dribble, maddened by dead heat, the terror that precedes it.
Los hombres: placeless place for castration. A horse opera
held outdoors goes to pieces in direct proportion with
slanted terrain.

Someone keeps it inside his body for a record time, you write later,
neither admiring nor—.

Dear X

Give it to me! To sing blackmail squeal, *Die Sprache*
der Mutter, under the law of repetition, foreign and blind
to itself like a fake coin in beggar's hand. Make yourself ugly,
you say, so men on the street won't—. I palm off the rest,
not in the mouth and counting to a hundred.

The viola of habit sounds its blue note, two of a kind,
barring the self. Intact milk factory.

There is no end to small talk in the wee hours.

Dear X

At night I cross the ratty park to tamper my nerves.
Always already the mean alleluia of slumped bodies,
citational protocol: those in favor nod aye, turncoats
flip

their asses above ground level as if self-variance were a vogue,
marquee approval at last.

You and I do nothing without corresponding anatomy in place:
his clit here, my guess——. We cake the ice and leak
the files in a fit of pique with split infinitive, bullwhip
pronouns on the hoof.

Dear X

Do you remember my falling period? This, then, is an orphaned frame
of reference like the all-girl band on the hit parade, pencil-slim
rail in case they head downward, nylons and slide guitar deep in the eye.

To repeat the madhouse effect without leaning on daddy, (firearm
discharged in quick succession) I faint and will myself to suffer
a brief absence from the vamping room.

La folie du jour (madness of the day) returns at noon with models
and pins. You wash your hands of any possible identification.
In the john, I nag. *The Slits* open for *Vertical Pillows*.

Dear X

Sounds like an invitation. Without giving to think
you've made the cut. Blipped breasts stall letterbox
appeal. If there is any, it follows partial objects home.
I have a great desire to strip these specular zones down
to craft. The materiality of Y gets in the way.

That would be career day: bring your daughters to court.

Trim nails and skip town just as the proverbial pang
of regret goes off the air. Speaking through the grid,
I opt for a tall blond with caved-in chest, déjà vu
drag shading into blue.

Dear X

Hold on! Let's talk about the one who goes out at night, A ritual
of sorts. In my dream I push the envelope of captivity as if
I'd written it myself: "Dear X, don't let this informal address
trump you..."

Why is it you've dressed this compound sentence for discredit?
Have you forgotten restrictions on trains and buses are on the rise?
A better subtitle would stray from browbeating the reader.

Precisely. When yellow and white stripes fan out in the distance,
I boot up: like in a flip book, a man with a loaf of bread appears
on the screen. Scroll, click, you're dead. There's the street
of crocodiles cordoned off at each end.

Dear X

That's why the slum series neither flattens nor puffs up.
A single prompt and they will seize its lack of fiction
as if crossing a traffic island. Having been there done that,
the cafeteria girl skims 10% off the top.

She is in the zone now with reps and a double-dip charge.
Strictly speaking, a set of mug shots lies between her score
and quitting time: eye pushed to the front insofar
as X implies Y. Endocrine problem nonobstant.

When the shit hits the fan, who will be crushed or pinked
with holes in the doo-wop morning?

Dear X

I have trouble with the standard notion of agency.
Which comes down to an all-purpose cramp on my second shift:
skid (off) snuff (out) pitfall as the phrase goes.

How's my driving? I mean writing. I do have license
to shoulder oblivion. Implacable medallion on the rack,
escalating rhetoric in the long run. It won't keep me
from panic around the edges.

Admit it! The least one can say your manner is negative
as if cancelling out a word resists momentary death,
sticking a landing deep in a hole.

To keep under wraps, the vanity of the apparatus.
What do we want? PUSSY! When do we want it? —!
Tout the ticket: (enter password) that suspends the loss.

Dear X

Face it! You haven't—in ages.
The deadbeat dad calls out for sushi & beer
while I go out on a limb. Tomorrow

we memorize colloquial expressions having to do
with sex, in the strict sense, scum, lily pads
nipped in the bud. A mob becomes part of a current

that sucks them in and how could the prohibition
not apply here, within an inch of her life, pass through
the noose, *comme une lettre à la poste?*

Dear X

Aren't we ready yet? Framing device, portapak?
pratfall plausibility of forgetting? We pluck
coins from the eyes of the dead for all to see
this forged precision we make like an empty
hospital bed: material tears

now lap dissolve apology, wide-angle pink sample
cued to kissing. Fuck the part!

Who'll walk the dog behind sexpot reservoir
where the package stands to die for?

Dear X

I could've told you it would end like this: breakass romp
through town with dogs out of their depths. *Escalator en panne.*
A kind of X that is not Y, prior to losing your head.

Malevolent eye-candy (one roll per envelope) on account of old
chestnut about repeating history, black rations and thug
vocabulary throwing her to the ground. Splatter footage
misses the point: hit rewind to search for dough.

Do not drill me about the function of collage: she hated
the sordid alignment of tenement windows, sitting on her hands
at halftime as if the live crowd might delete her own sound
screen out dumb trick in taxicab while you hum a few bars.

Dear X

Nor is it all. After replacement therapy he stands
on his dignity while she shoots off her mouth an edge
to her voice like some kind of abattoir about to collapse

human vitrine large glass a file

the minute you divine its wraparound structure you begin
your descent in the chatty anonymity toward the cut
boarded up for now by fake interiors and steel brackets.

Unversed in the dialectic of the hole you call it rupture
of desire indiscreet gap open to view as if any old sewers
were conduit enough into the city's black lung heart
wolfman at a pauper's grave

Dear X

Speaking of slander, your clandestine bid did not go
unnoticed. In the double driveway the queen's laughter
singles me out, like a hand-held camera, I approach the bar:

Pink ribbons, bannister, odor di femina

"I'll bring my little girl for a swim!"

Sweet daisy wheel pounds at the abhorrence.

Should you remain without news of me holed up in the morass,
it would not do to film behind the pier. See the rope, absolute
drag, that loop in the river. Someone's dying to lop it off
as if he were a doctor or land surveyor inverting the flow,
remapping the lot.

As if gender's corset had not been hung to dry.

)Tombeaux(

once barbarous and
                    external

matter

now

        moral

and within us

—Stéphane Mallarmé

Tombeau 1 for Sarah Kofman (1935–1994)

to inherit the vanished
you hear the shofar's sorrow

roundup volume
at the Vel d'Hiv

wearing the star
for the charnel house

terror o lullaby
in someone else's hand

that lists all six of us

Tombeau II for Paul Celan (1920–1970)

to enter Hades do not go near the smokestacks
stammer far apart trauma's other name
saving yourself the cost of missing tongue
where every appearance of forgiving is washed
clean, cast to the winds, an amulet
strapped to the left arm

memory's glove has brought you here
to this cul-de-sac most likely to collapse
at the faultline irreproachable prayers
narrow your eyes, invert letters
all is well for the deaf and dumb
death sends her regards

Tombeau III for Bruno Schulz (1892–1942)

to have done with
the day's account

do not shower just yet
in tomorrow's lap

where the street ends
someone has drawn

would-be stumps deeply cut
golem said to rewrite

history's slogan, if only
you could read the wretched

meaning of the eternal, beat him
to the punch, this fata morgana

this lurid self-parody
in the cinnamon shop

would surrender its rotten spread

Tombeau IV for Walter Benjamin (1892–1940)

outside the camps you dream the dream of passing
from text to text a yes-or-no night summons its guard
little open-air theatre few are admitted to without recanting
strange tense agreement   had he been...he would have...

in the dictionary of impossibilities a man looks up surviving
strictly forbidden by his clan: do not answer little hunchback's
greeting asleep in an overcoat too light for the season.
Penny ante dawn, do not mention the irregular conjugation, old
cortège of double-binds abandoned at last.

The quoted passage could be a translation, faulty at that

Tombeau V for Edmond Jabès (1912–1991)

out of her mind Sarah
screams your dream a book

of ashes irrevocably lost
in a dress of parts condemned

to writing the shapes of words
yet to come will not return

the deported lovers summed up
elsewhere trace a wide margin

the desert disperses with each new telling
you should have turned the page, Yukel

else pitched your tent apart
from the source of torment

Tombeau VI for Robert Desnos (1900 –1945)

to be late for one's own death rehearsal
to hell with pall-bearers pumping iron in uniform

put a phonograph on my tomb you said
as if life was a waltz, mechanical ballet, scream

on a train from Fresnes to Compiègnes a sleep cantata
with strings, blows and the voiceless noise between stops

that is not the proper sequence: Interior. Night. Cattlecar.
Syntax is robbed of its function: any order will do

Auschwitz Buchenwald Theresienstadt. Slowly we are getting
nowhere in the open space after a name: here lies

Tombeau VII for Max Jacob (1876-1944)

like a leather cup before dawn you throw
your hands up. Death is at the door.

On a canal a rooming house or laundry boat
bites the hand that writes the score. Once you lived

in full attire jacked up by your lack of rhyme.
To lose balance now would tip them off, let

the tulle curtains down. Hello, night on earth,
au revoir, les enfants. A patch of fur or yellow star

stretches out across the Seine. The sentence we need here
goes plunk like a bald soprano before the convoy

pushes off again from its muddy bed

Tombeau VIII for Jerzy Kosinski (1933–1991)

strained through fear the last straw
retains blood at the rim you tear

your gaze from being there to collar
the rumor against your skin, to check

appropriate box in the catalogue of death

Tombeau IX for Primo Levi (1919–1987)

down there concentrationnaire
Lager's ghosts
slip from the column, soup poles
heavy with snow

begin counting by five
piles of silver spoons, stacks
of corpses you mistake for wood

Polish still life: snow   rubble
bodies intent on telling what they saw
draw horses, your own conclusion
screaming in a pasture

here's your registration from hell
worn on the inside
of the arm, *anus mundi*
untellable, still

Tombeau X for Klara Kopilewicz (1909–2000)

to read the heart monitor
do not check out of the room

I prefer language's razor—tiny kvetch bird—
to the sound of pills crushed into powder

in a bed of veins there is waiting
sewn together like an ivy cuff, impractical

image no one understands the accent
falls on the first syllable

as if death
upon reaching morning signed her name

in blue ashes on graph paper

Chris Tysh, born and educated in Paris, was naturalized as a citizen of the United States on July 4th, 1998 at Chene Park in Detroit. She teaches creative writing and women's studies at Wayne State University. Her books include *Secrets of Elegance, Porne, Coat of Arms* and *In the Name. Car men, a play in d* premiered at The Detroit Institute of Arts, November 15, 1996. She is currently working on a film script based on the work of Georges Bataille.

La Foire des Femmes, Paris, 1972

This book was typeset in Perpetua designed by Eric Gill and Big Girl Ultra Bold designed by Susan LaPorte. Printed in a trade edition of 1000 copies by Cushing-Malloy in Ann Arbor, Michigan. 26 copies lettered A–Z are signed by the author.

Other Books from United Artists

Nothing for You by Ted Berrigan $12.00
Judyism by Jim Brodey $8.00
The California Papers by Steve Carey $8.00
Personal Effects by Charlotte Carter $7.00
The Fox by Jack Collom $8.00
Columbus Square Journal by William Corbett $7.00
Smoking in the Twilight Bar by Barbara Henning $7.00
Love Makes Thinking Dark by Barbara Henning $7.00
Head by Bill Kushner $7.00
Love Uncut by Bill Kushner $7.00
That April by Bill Kushner $10.00
One at a Time by Gary Lenhart $7.00
Another Smashed Pinecone by Bernadette Mayer $10.00
Eruditio Ex Memoria by Bernadette Mayer $8.00
Something to Hold Onto by Dennis Moritz $8.00
Songs from the Unborn Second Baby by Alice Notley $10.00
Fool Consciousness by Liam O'Gallagher $7.00
Cleaning Up New York by Bob Rosenthal $8.00
Political Conditions/Physical States by Tom Savage $7.00
In the Heart of the Empire by Harris Schiff $8.00
Along the Rails by Elio Schneeman $8.00
Echolalia by George Tysh $8.00
Selected Poems by Charlie Vermont $7.00
Blue Mosque by Anne Waldman $8.00
Information from the Surface of Venus by Lewis Warsh $8.00
The Maharajah's Son by Lewis Warsh $10.00
The Fast by Hannah Weiner $8.00

United Artists Books
112 Milton Street
Brooklyn, NY 11222